1854

KIRSTEN'S COOK BOOK

*A Peek at
Dining in the
Past with Meals
You Can Cook Today*

PLEASANT COMPANY PUBLICATIONS, INC.

First Edition.
Printed in the United States of America.
94 95 96 97 98 99 WCR 10 9 8 7 6 5 4 3 2

PICTURE CREDITS
The following individuals and organizations have generously
given permission to reprint illustrations in this book:
Page 1—*Early Family Home*, Crabtree Publishing Company, 350 Fifth Ave., Suite 3308,
New York, NY, 10118; 2—Nordiska Museet (top); Photograph, Judith Sandoval,
© 1986, Bonanza Group Incorporated (bottom left); *Early Farm Life*, Crabtree
Publishing Company, 350 Fifth Ave., Suite 3308, New York, NY, 10118 (bottom right);
3—The American Swedish Institute/Minneapolis, Minnesota (top); North Wind
Picture Archives (bottom); 11—From the Collection of the Minnesota Historical
Society (bottom); 13—Old World Wisconsin, Eagle, WI; 14—State Historical Society
of Wisconsin; 17—State Historical Society of Wisconsin; 19—Courtesy Library of
Congress (top); 20—*Food for the Settler*, Crabtree Publishing Company, 350 Fifth Ave.,
Suite 3308, New York, NY, 10118; 21—*Early Farm Life*, Crabtree Publishing Company,
350 Fifth Ave., Suite 3308, New York, NY, 10118; 22—Suhr Farmstead,
Dodge County, WI; 25—Everett B. Wilson; 27—State Historical Society of Wisconsin;
30—*Early Settler Children*, Crabtree Publishing Company, 350 Fifth Ave.,
Suite 3308, New York, NY, 10118; 31—State Historical Society of Wisconsin;
33—*Early Farm Life*, Crabtree Publishing Company, 350 Fifth Ave., Suite 3308, New
York, NY, 10118 (top); California Museum of Photography, Keystone-Mast Collection,
University of Riverside, California (bottom); 37—Nordiska Museet (top); *Early Family
Home*, Crabtree Publishing Company, 350 Fifth Ave., Suite 3308, New York, NY, 10118
(bottom); 41—Nordiska Museet (bottom); 42—*Early Farm Life*,
Crabtree Publishing Company, 350 Fifth Ave., Suite 3308, New York, NY, 10118;
43—Wadsworth Atheneum, Hartford. The Ella Gallup Sumner
and Mary Catlin Sumner Collection Fund.

Edited by Jodi Evert and Jeanne Thieme
Written by Terri Braun, Jodi Evert, and Jeanne Thieme
Designed and Art Directed by Jane S. Varda
Produced by Karen Bennett, Laura Paulini, and Pat Tuchscherer
Cover Illustration by Renée Graef
Inside Illustrations by Susan Mahal
Photography by Mark Salisbury
Historical and Picture Research by Polly Athan, Rebecca Sample Bernstein,
Terri Braun, Jodi Evert, Robyn Hansen, and Doreen Smith
Recipe Testing Coordinated by Jean doPico
Food Styling by Janice Bell
Prop Research by Leslie Cakora

Library of Congress Cataloging-in-Publication Data
Kirsten's cookbook : a peek at dining in the past with meals
you can cook today. — 1st ed.
p. cm. — (The American girls collection)
ISBN 1-56247-111-2 (pbk.)
1. Cookery—Juvenile literature. 2. Cookery, American—Juvenile literature. 3. United
States—Social life and customs—19th century—Juvenile literature. [1. Cookery,
American. 2. United States—Social life and customs—19th century.]
I. Series

CONTENTS

Special thanks to all the children and adults who tested the recipes and gave us their valuable comments:

Emily Ballweg and her mother Amy Ballweg
Amelia Barber and her mother Gale Barber
Meredith Barbera and her mother Cindy Barbera
Elizabeth Beetem and her mother Anne Beetem
Whitney Bembenek and her mother Debbi Bembenek
Rebeccah Biser and her father David Biser
Abbey Bollig and her mother Julie Bollig
Michelle Bridge and her mother Becky Bridge
Alisa Brown and her mother Marlene Brown
Katie Bush and her mother Kathryn Bush
Sarah Louise Campbell and her mother Judy Campbell
Ashleigh Conrad and her mother Glenda Conrad
Stephanie Cox and her mother Lori Cox
Cassie Dabel and her mother Ginny Dabel
Emily Dresen and her mother Mary Jo Dresen
Katie Dryburgh and her mother Nancy Dryburgh
Jenna Eddington and her mother Sheri Eddington
Stephanie Endres and her mother Alice Endres
Michelle Endres and her mother Brenda Endres
Kelly Fitzpatrick and her mother Judith Fitzpatrick
Angela Fraser and her mother Janet Wells
Larissa Frymark and her mother Mary Frymark

COOKING ON THE FRONTIER

Cooking and dining were more than pastimes for American girls long ago. On the Minnesota frontier in 1854, making the family's meals was the biggest job girls and women had. Every day, Kirsten Larson worked with her mother in their tiny log cabin. She fed wood to the fire in the cookstove and hauled water from the creek when it was time to wash dishes.

Pioneer families like Kirsten's ate what they could grow on their frontier farms or gather in the woods nearby. There were no supermarkets in 1854. Instead, pioneers planted and harvested their own grain for bread and cereal. They got milk, butter, and cheese from cows or goats they raised themselves. Eggs came from their own chickens. For meat, they butchered animals that they raised or hunted or trapped.

In winter, when the hens stopped laying eggs and the cows didn't give milk, pioneer families didn't have those foods to eat. Kirsten and Mama cooked foods like bread and potatoes again and again because the ingredients were common on the frontier. They rarely planned special meals because time for preparing them was scarce. But sometimes there were treats—especially on holidays.

Learning about kitchens and cooking in the past will help you understand what it was like to grow up the way Kirsten did. Cooking the foods she ate in your own kitchen will help bring history alive for you and your family.

KIRSTEN ♥ 1854

Kirsten Larson was a pioneer. She lived in a one-room log cabin on the Minnesota frontier. Kirsten and her family came from Sweden. When immigrants made new homes for themselves in America, they didn't forget the recipes and customs of their homeland.

PIONEER KITCHENS

PIONEER PANTRIES

Pioneers didn't have electric refrigerators. They often kept the day's milk and butter in a **pantry**. *Sometimes a pantry was a small room where bread and preserved foods were also stored. In a one-room log cabin like Kirsten's, the pantry might have been a few shelves in a corner of the cabin.*

ROOT CELLARS

Pioneers built root cellars to keep some vegetables and fruits cool and dry. They dug a hole in the ground under their cabin or into a nearby hillside. Potatoes, apples, cabbages, and carrots usually didn't freeze underground, even during the coldest Minnesota winters.

The Larsons ate in the kitchen—which was also the dining room, the living room, and the only bedroom in their one-room log cabin! The cookstove heated the cabin. In winter months, it was nice to have the table near the hot cookstove. But when the weather was warmer, the little cabin got very hot and stuffy whenever Kirsten and Mama cooked.

The cookstove did not have on/off switches or knobs marked "low," "medium," and "high." If Mama needed lots of heat on top of the stove, she burned dry oak or another hardwood. If she wanted to bake something slowly, she used less wood, or green wood, or a softer wood like birch, to keep the oven temperature lower. One of the first things Kirsten learned about cooking was how to feed the fire in the stove. Mama passed along hints for judging oven temperatures. For example, the oven was just right for baking bread when Kirsten could hold her bare hand inside the oven for as long as it took to count to 20, but no longer.

There was no running water in log cabins like Kirsten's. Children often had the job of bringing water from the well or a nearby stream. Cleanup was one of the hardest things about frontier cooking. Pans of dishwater had to be heated on the cookstove. Pioneers washed dishes with soap made from lard and *lye*, which came from stove ashes. Sometimes they scrubbed burned pans with sand or with brushes they made from twigs.

SETTING KIRSTEN'S TABLE

There were no matching dishes on Kirsten's table. The Larsons thought they were lucky to have enough cups, forks, and knives so that no one had to share!

Swedish kitchen utensils and storage containers.

Some of the plates and bowls the Larsons used came all the way from Sweden. A few were borrowed from Aunt Inger. Papa bought one metal plate at the general store in town. He and Lars, Kirsten's older brother, carved the rest from wood. They carved wooden spoons for cooking and eating, too.

Mama wove beautiful linen cloth on her loom, but often there wasn't a tablecloth on the smooth wooden table. Pioneers like the Larsons rarely used napkins, either. Laundry was a difficult chore, so cloth napkins were not practical. Paper ones hadn't been invented yet in 1854.

SWEDISH TABLE GRACE

At meals, children were expected to be seen and not heard. A young girl like Kirsten might not speak at all, except to say grace along with Papa. The Larsons might have used this prayer before each meal. It means, "May God bless the food we eat."

Välsigna Gud den mat vi få.
Vel-SING-nuh Goodt den maht vee foh.

TIPS FOR TODAY'S COOKS

You'll find below a list of things that every good cook should know. But this is the most important tip: **work with an adult.** This is the safe way for you to work in the kitchen. Cooking together is fun, too. It's a tradition American families have always shared. Keep it alive today!

MEASURING FLOUR

A good cook measures exactly. Here is a hint for measuring flour. Spoon the flour into a measuring cup, heaping it up over the top. Then use the spoon handle to level off the flour. Don't shake or tap the cup.

TABLE OF MEASUREMENTS

3 teaspoons = 1 tablespoon
2 cups = 1 pint
2 pints = 1 quart
4 cups = 1 quart

1. Choose a time that suits you and the adult who's cooking with you, so that you will both enjoy working together in the kitchen.

2. Wash your hands with soap before and after you handle food. Wear an apron, tie back your hair, and roll up your sleeves.

3. Read a recipe carefully, all the way through, before you start it. Look at the pictures. They will help you understand the steps.

4. Gather all the ingredients and equipment you will need before you start to cook. Put everything where you can reach it easily.

5. Ask an adult to show you how to peel, cut, and grate with sharp kitchen tools. Always use a chopping board to save kitchen counters.

6. Pay attention while using knives so that you don't cut your fingers! Remember—a good, sharp knife is safer than a dull one.

7. When you stir or mix, hold the bowl or pan steady on a flat surface, not in your arms.

8. Make sure your mixing bowls, pots, and pans are the right size. If they are too small, you'll probably spill. If pots and pans are too large, foods will burn more easily.

9. Clean up spills right away.

10. Pots and pans will be less likely to spill on the stove if you turn the handles toward the side.

11. Have an adult handle hot pans. Don't use the stove burners or the oven without permission or supervision.

12. Turn off the burner or the oven as soon as a dish is cooked.

13. Potholders and oven mitts will protect you from burns. Use them when you touch anything hot. Protect kitchen counters by putting trivets or cooling racks under hot pots and pans.

14. Keep hot foods hot and cold foods cold. If you plan to make things early and serve them later, store them properly. Foods that could spoil belong in the refrigerator. Wrap foods well.

15. If you decide to make a whole meal, be sure to plan so that all the food will be ready when you are ready to serve it.

16. Cleanup is part of cooking, too. Leave the kitchen at least as clean as you found it. Wash all the dishes, pots, and pans. Sweep the floor. Throw away the garbage.

RECIPES IN THE 1850s

There were no standard-sized measuring cups and spoons in the 1850s. So recipes told cooks to add a "pinch" of salt, a "thimbleful" of cinnamon, a "dust" of flour, a "squeeze" of lemon, a "handful" of rice, or a lump of butter "the size of an egg."

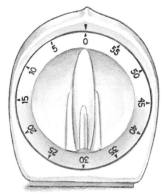

TIMING

When a recipe gives two cooking times—for example, when it says, "bake 25 to 30 minutes"—first set the timer for the shorter time. If the food is not done when the timer rings, give it more time.

BREAKFAST

A cookstove.

O n frosty fall mornings, Kirsten woke up before sunrise to the sound of Papa or Mama putting wood in the cast-iron cookstove. The crackle and pop of burning wood could be as loud as any alarm clock!

Kirsten didn't wait in bed until she heard the sizzle of frying sausage or sniffed the aroma of coffee boiling on the stove. She got up right away because she had a job to do. It was time to help Mama cook breakfast—the hearty meal that started a hungry pioneer family's day.

Kirsten went straight to the stove. If it was so cold that she could see her breath inside the cabin, she stopped for a moment to wrap a shawl around her shoulders. She wore it until the cookstove made the whole cabin toasty warm.

As Papa and the boys fed the animals, Kirsten and Mama fed wood to the stove so that they could fry fresh pork sausage and boil eggs and coffee. Creamy rice porridge was a special breakfast treat that was waiting in the oven. Kirsten and Mama had made the porridge the day before, and it had stayed warm overnight beside a low-burning fire in the oven. The bread had been baked days earlier and stored on shelves.

BREAKFAST

♥

Pork Sausage Patties

•

Hard-Boiled Eggs

•

Swedish Rice Porridge

•

Round Rye Bread

•

Homemade Butter

•

Ginger Cookies

One food that Kirsten ate is not often seen on breakfast tables today. She topped off her meal with a cookie, and then slipped another into her pocket for a mid-morning snack. Dinner at noon was a long way off!

PORK SAUSAGE PATTIES

Allspice, ginger, and cloves add a Swedish flavor to these pork sausage patties.

INGREDIENTS

1½ pounds lean
   ground pork
½ teaspoon salt
½ teaspoon pepper
½ teaspoon allspice
¼ teaspoon cloves
¼ teaspoon ginger

EQUIPMENT

Mixing bowl
Measuring spoons
Mixing spoon
Heavy 10-inch skillet
Spatula
Ovenproof plate and foil

DIRECTIONS   *12 patties*

1. Put the pork into the mixing bowl. Add the salt, pepper, allspice, cloves, and ginger. Stir the ingredients with the mixing spoon.

2. Divide the mixture into 12 equal portions on a clean countertop. Roll each portion into a ball and flatten it to make a patty.

3. Place the skillet over medium heat for 1 minute. Arrange 6 sausage patties in the skillet. Let them cook for 3 or 4 minutes.

4. Turn the patties and cook them for 4 minutes more. Both sides should be golden brown.

5. Put the cooked patties on the ovenproof plate and cover them with foil. Put the plate in a warm (200°) oven.

6. Have an adult remove any extra grease from the skillet. Then cook the remaining 6 patties, following steps 3 through 5. ♥

BUTCHERING

*Almost every pioneer family had at least one hog to **butcher**, or kill and cut up, in the late fall. They used every part of the animal. Pigskin was tanned to make leather. Bristles made brushes. Brains were fried in lard and eaten as a breakfast treat.*

HARD-BOILED EGGS

INGREDIENTS
6 large eggs
Cold water
Salt and pepper

EQUIPMENT
1-quart saucepan with lid
Kitchen towel
Knife

Pioneer children often had the job of gathering eggs, a good breakfast food the family enjoyed when the hens were laying.

DIRECTIONS *6 servings*

1. Put the eggs into the saucepan and cover them with cold water.

2. Place the pan over medium heat. Bring the water to a *boil*. When water boils, big bubbles rise to the top and burst.

3. Turn off the heat and put the lid on the pan. Remove the pan from the burner and let the eggs stand, covered, for 15 minutes. Then remove the lid.

4. Have an adult take the pan to the sink and place it under cold running water. When the water is completely cool, remove the eggs.

5. Dry the shells and place 1 egg on each plate at the breakfast table.

6. Shell your egg at the table, the way Kirsten did. Then cut the egg in slices and season it with salt and pepper. ♥

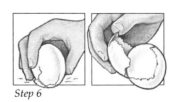

Step 6

SWEDISH RICE PORRIDGE

*Rice porridge, known as **Skånsk gröt** in Sweden, made pioneer settlers like Kirsten feel at home in America.*

INGREDIENTS

1 large, firm apple
1 teaspoon butter
1 cup white rice
1 cup water
3-inch cinnamon stick
4 cups milk
3 tablespoons brown sugar
1/3 cup raisins
1 teaspoon vanilla
Cream
Honey

EQUIPMENT

Paring knife
Cutting board
Measuring cups
  and spoons
3-quart saucepan with lid
Wooden spoon
Serving bowl

DIRECTIONS   *6 servings*

1. Have an adult help you cut the apple into 4 sections.

Step 2

2. Use the paring knife to cut away the core and peel the skin from the apple. Chop the apple into small pieces on the cutting board. Set the apple aside.

3. Use your fingers to rub butter over the bottom of the saucepan. The butter will keep the rice from sticking while it cooks.

4. Put the rice, water, and cinnamon stick into the saucepan. Place the pan on the stove over medium heat.

5. Bring the mixture to a *boil*. Large bubbles will rise to the top and burst when the mixture boils.

6. Lower the heat until the mixture *simmers*. You will see tiny bubbles along the edge of the pan when it is simmering.

7. Cover the pan and simmer the rice 10 to 15 minutes, or until the water has been absorbed.

8. Pour the milk into the saucepan. Turn up the heat and stir until it begins to simmer.

9. When the milk begins to simmer, turn down the heat to low. Carefully add the brown sugar, chopped apple, and raisins. Stir gently.

10. Cover the pan and allow the porridge to simmer for about 45 minutes. As it cooks, it will thicken. Stir it once or twice as it cooks.

11. Turn off the heat and take the pan from the stove. Remove the cinnamon stick. Stir in the vanilla.

12. Pour the porridge into a bowl. Serve it warm with cream or honey. Or, if you make the porridge ahead of time, put it in the refrigerator and warm it up again before you serve it. ♥

SKÅNSK GRÖT

Pioneers bought rice, sugar, and spices at the store to make Skånsk gröt (SKONE-sk groot). Then they added apples that grew nearby and raisins dried from wild grapes. Skånsk gröt was often cooked for dessert. Leftovers were kept warm in the oven overnight for a special breakfast treat.

WILD RICE

This Indian woman is harvesting wild rice just as women from the Ojibwa and Dakota tribes did in Kirsten's time. Wild rice was a very important food for these American Indian tribes. In 1854, the flavor of wild rice wasn't popular with most settlers. They often bought white rice in frontier stores instead.

ROUND RYE BREAD

*"She who has baked a good batch of bread
has done a good day's work."*
–Old American saying

INGREDIENTS

¾ cup milk
2 tablespoons soft butter
½ cup lukewarm water
2 packages dry yeast
½ cup dark brown sugar
1 tablespoon ground
    fennel seed
1 teaspoon salt
1 cup white flour
3 cups rye flour
1 tablespoon vegetable oil
Extra oil and rye flour
Extra butter

EQUIPMENT

Measuring cups
    and spoons
Small saucepan
Butter knife
Wooden spoon
Large mixing bowl
Kitchen towel
Cookie sheet
Fork
Potholders
Wire cooling rack

HOMEMADE YEAST

*Pioneer cooks made their own yeast
starter by mixing flour, sugar, salt, and
warm potato water. Then they let the
mixture **ferment**, or grow, for several
days. On baking day, they used some of
their starter to make bread. A good yeast
starter was highly prized and could last
for years.*

DIRECTIONS   *1 loaf*

1. Put the milk into the saucepan and begin to
   warm it over low heat. As the milk warms, cut
   the butter into small pieces and add them to
   the milk. Stir to help the butter melt. Then turn
   off the heat.

2. Measure the lukewarm water into the mixing
   bowl. Sprinkle the yeast over the water. Stir
   well. Set the bowl aside for 5 minutes.

3. Add the milk and melted butter to the yeast
   mixture. Stir in the brown sugar, fennel, and
   salt. Add the white flour, and stir to mix
   the ingredients.

HOW TO KNEAD DOUGH

1. Push the heels of your hands down into the dough and away from you.

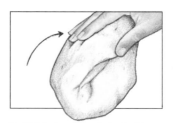

2. Fold the dough in half.

3. Turn the dough.

4. Push the dough again. Repeat these steps. They will soon become simple, and your kneading will have a rhythm.

4. Gradually mix in 2 cups of the rye flour. The dough will be very stiff and sticky. Add enough of the remaining rye flour so that you can shape the dough into a ball. Do not add all of the remaining flour. You'll need some for step 6.

5. Cover the mixing bowl with a towel and let the dough rest in a warm spot for 10 or 15 minutes.

6. Take the dough out of the bowl and place it on a table or counter that has been sprinkled with some of the remaining flour. Dust your hands with flour and knead the dough. Whenever the dough begins to stick to your hands, dust them with more flour and sprinkle a little more flour on the dough. By the time you have used the last of the flour, the dough should not be sticky.

7. After 5 to 10 minutes of kneading, you will have a smooth ball of dough. If you have kneaded the dough enough, it will spring back when you poke it with your finger. ➡

FLAT BREADS

Pioneer women made flat breads by rolling bread dough into thin sheets. Sometimes they stored flat breads by hanging them from the cabin rafters.

Step 9

8. Cover the dough with the towel and let it rest while you wash and dry the mixing bowl.

9. Coat the inside of the bowl with oil. Put the dough into the bowl. Roll it around until it is completely coated with oil to keep it from drying out and cracking as it rises. Cover the bowl with the towel and set it in a warm, draft-free place to rise.

10. After about 45 minutes, check the dough. It should be twice as big as it was before rising. If your dough hasn't doubled in size after 45 minutes, give it more time. Check it again every 15 minutes.

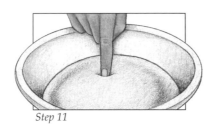

Step 11

11. When the dough has doubled in size, test it by poking it with your finger. If the dough does not spring back, it is ready to be shaped.

12. Oil the cookie sheet. Sprinkle it with a little rye flour.

13. Punch the dough in the bowl once or twice to remove the air. Then knead it a few times.

BREAD OVENS

Some pioneers had both indoor and outdoor bread ovens. In the winter, they baked their bread in ovens built into their fireplaces to help heat their cabins. The outdoor oven shown in this picture is just like the ovens pioneers used in the 1850s. They used the outdoor oven in the summer to keep the heat out of their homes.

14. Shape the dough into a round loaf about 7 inches across. This is a traditional Swedish shape for bread. Place it on the cookie sheet, cover it with the towel, and let it rise again for 45 minutes.

15. Preheat the oven to 375°. Pierce the top of the loaf with a fork to keep it from cracking as it bakes. Make a deeper hole in the center by rotating the fork.

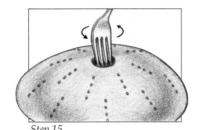
Step 15

16. Place the cookie sheet on the middle rack of the oven. Bake the bread for 50 to 60 minutes. When the top is brown, have an adult tap the top of the loaf. If it sounds hollow, the bread is done. Have an adult remove it from the oven and place it on the rack to cool.

17. While the loaf is still warm—but not hot enough to burn you—rub the top with butter. After 2 or 3 hours, the bread will be cool enough to slice. ♥

From the book *Kirsten's Surprise*

BAKING BREAD

At every meal, Swedish pioneers like the Larsons ate the same kinds of bread they had eaten in Sweden—dark, sturdy loaves of rye and hard, crisp flat breads. Kirsten and Mama baked as many as a dozen loaves at a time!

Homemade Butter

You don't need a churn to make enough rich, creamy butter for breakfast.

INGREDIENTS

2 cups *(1 pint)* heavy
 whipping cream, chilled
Pinch of salt

EQUIPMENT

2-quart jar with tight lid
1 marble
Strainer
2-quart bowl
Measuring cup
Wooden spoon
Butter mold or serving dish

DIRECTIONS *6 ounces*

1. Chill the jar and the marble in the refrigerator for at least 1 hour to help the butter form more quickly.

2. Place the strainer over the bowl. Set them aside.

3. Pour the cream into the jar, drop in the marble, and fasten the lid tight.

Step 4

4. Shake the jar. At first you will hear the marble moving. After about 15 minutes, the cream will get so thick that you won't hear or feel the marble. The sides of the jar will be coated with thick cream.

Step 5

5. Continue shaking the jar. After another 15 to 30 minutes, butter will begin to form. First you will hear the marble moving again. Then the coating of cream will disappear from the sides of the jar and you will see lumps of butter in a milky liquid. The liquid is buttermilk.

6. Open the jar and pour the butter and the buttermilk into the strainer. The buttermilk will flow into the bowl, and the butter will stay in the strainer.

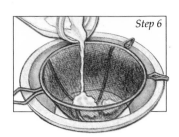

Step 6

7. Pour the buttermilk from the bowl into a covered container and store it in the refrigerator. You can drink the buttermilk or use it in another recipe, such as Swedish almond rusks *(page 26)*. Rinse the bowl with cold water to remove all the buttermilk.

8. Turn the butter out of the strainer and into the bowl. Cover the butter with cold water, and then pour the water off through the strainer. Do not save the milky water.

CHURNING BUTTER

*Pioneers in the 1850s made butter in a wooden butter churn, just as the woman in this picture is doing. The churn's **dasher**, or handle, moved up and down, beating the cream in the churn until it turned to butter. Sometimes women sold or traded butter for supplies they couldn't make, like sugar and spices.*

9. Keep washing the butter in this way until the water you pour off is clear. You are washing out the buttermilk. Buttermilk that is not washed out will turn the butter sour.

10. Use a clean wooden spoon to stir and press the butter against the side of the bowl. Continue pressing the butter against the side of the bowl to work out any liquid that is left in the butter. Pour it off.

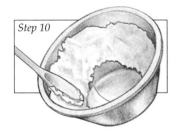

Step 10

11. If you like your butter lightly salted, add a pinch of salt and stir it in.

12. Press the butter into a dish or a butter mold. Chill it in the refrigerator for an hour before you serve it. ♥

GINGER COOKIES

*Kirsten ate these thick, spicy cookies
with hot milk sprinkled with cinnamon.*

INGREDIENTS

6 cups flour
2 teaspoons baking soda
1 teaspoon salt
1 teaspoon allspice
1 teaspoon ginger
1 teaspoon cloves
1 teaspoon cinnamon
1 cup brown sugar
$\frac{1}{3}$ cup soft shortening
$1\frac{1}{2}$ cups dark molasses
$\frac{2}{3}$ cup cold water
Shortening to grease baking sheets
Extra flour for rolling out dough

EQUIPMENT

Flour sifter
2 large mixing bowls
Measuring cups
 and spoons
Wooden spoon
Large plate
Cookie sheets
Rolling pin
Cookie cutter
Spatula
Potholders

DIRECTIONS   *2½ dozen*

Step 1

1. Put the flour sifter into 1 large mixing bowl. Measure the flour, baking soda, salt, allspice, ginger, cloves, and cinnamon into the sifter. Then sift them into the bowl. Set the bowl aside.

2. Measure the brown sugar by packing it tightly into the measuring cup. Put it into the other large mixing bowl.

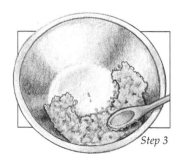

Step 3

3. Add the shortening to the brown sugar. Use the wooden spoon to press the brown sugar and shortening together against the side of the bowl. Then stir quickly until the mixture is creamy.

4. Add the molasses and water. Stir to mix well.

5. Add the sifted dry ingredients 1 cup at a time. Mix well after each addition. Keep mixing until all of the dry ingredients are mixed in.

6. Cover the bowl with a large plate. Chill the dough for 1 hour to make it easier to handle.

7. Preheat the oven to 350°. Grease the cookie sheets with shortening.

8. Sprinkle some flour onto a table or counter and cover the rolling pin with flour to keep the dough from sticking. Use more flour when you need it.

9. Divide the dough into four sections. Roll out the first section from the center of the dough to the edges. Try to keep the whole piece 1/2 inch thick.

10. Cut out circles with the cookie cutter. Lift the cookies onto a cookie sheet with the spatula. Leave at least 2 inches between cookies, because they get big and puffy as they bake. Make more cookies from the rest of the dough, including the scraps.

11. Bake the cookies 12 to 15 minutes. Have an adult touch the cookies lightly. If touching leaves no imprint, the cookies are done.

12. Have an adult use the spatula to remove the cookies from the cookie sheets to cool. Don't stack the cookies if they are hot, or they will stick together. ❤

LARD

*There was no margarine or vegetable shortening in 1854. Pioneers cooked with **lard**, a shortening made from hog fat. This picture shows a woman melting down, or **rendering**, hog fat just as Kirsten and Mama had to do. The fat hardened when it cooled. Pioneers spread it on bread like butter.*

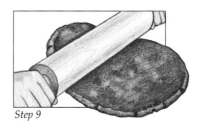

Step 9

BAKING SODA

*When Kirsten was a girl, baking soda was called **saleratus** (sal-a-RATE-us). Cooks used saleratus in cookies and quick breads instead of yeast, which needs long rising times. But saleratus could not be made at home like yeast. Pioneers had to buy or trade for it at the store.*

DINNER

A girl peeling potatoes.

Dinner in the early afternoon was the biggest meal of the day for the Larsons. Everyone was hungry after a morning of hard work in the fields, in the barn, in the garden, and in the cabin. The Larsons needed the extra energy they got from a big meal so they could continue working hard until the sun went down.

Kirsten and Mama began to prepare dinner as soon as they finished breakfast cleanup. As Mama began her morning chores in the barn, Kirsten went outside to tend the family garden.

First she pulled the weeds. Then she dug potatoes and pulled up an onion for the creamy Swedish potatoes Mama would fry in a big skillet on top of the cookstove. Finally, Kirsten cut a fresh head of cabbage.

Then Kirsten went back to the cabin to grate the cabbage and apples from the root cellar for a crisp salad. Mama brought in a thick ham slice from the smokehouse to bake in the oven. For dessert, Mama cooked her special fruit soup with dried apples, plums, grapes, and berries that Kirsten and Peter had picked and dried in the sun. Kirsten had helped Mama make Swedish almond rusks on baking day. They were stored on shelves and ready to eat with the fruit soup.

All of Kirsten's family members were expected to eat everything on their plates. But if there were any leftovers that could not be saved to eat later, one of Kirsten's chores was to feed the table scraps to the chickens and hogs. Nothing went to waste on a pioneer farm!

DINNER

♥

Baked Ham Slice

·

Swedish Potatoes

·

Cabbage and Apple Salad

·

Fruit Soup

·

Swedish Almond Rusks

BAKED HAM SLICE

*Ginger adds a Swedish flavor
to a juicy baked ham slice.*

INGREDIENTS

Smoked ham slice, fully
   cooked, $1/2$ inch thick
$1/4$ cup brown sugar
$1/2$ teaspoon ground ginger
Pinch of black pepper

EQUIPMENT

Cutting board
Sharp knife
Ungreased baking dish
Measuring cup and spoons
Small bowl and spoon
Potholders
Large plate or platter

DIRECTIONS   *4 to 6 servings*

1. Preheat the oven to 325°.

2. Have an adult help you trim away the fat
from the outside edge of the ham slice.

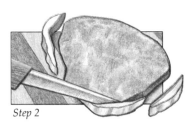

Step 2

3. Place the ham slice into the ungreased
baking dish.

4. Mix the brown sugar, ginger, and pepper
together in the small bowl.

5. Sprinkle all the sugar and spices evenly over
the top of the ham slice.

6. Bake the ham slice uncovered on the middle
rack in the oven for 30 minutes.

7. Have an adult remove the ham slice from the
oven and cut it into individual pieces. Serve
on a large plate or platter. ❤

SMOKING MEAT

*Pioneer families did not have electric
refrigerators or freezers. So after they
butchered animals, pioneers often
preserved, or **cured**, the meat by smoking
it. Sometimes they built **smokehouses**
similar to the one shown in this picture to
cure many pounds of meat at one time. A
ham might take four or five days to cure.*

SWEDISH POTATOES

INGREDIENTS

1 medium onion
6 medium potatoes
2 tablespoons shortening
1 teaspoon salt
1/2 teaspoon pepper
1 3/4 cups heavy cream,
   or half-and-half

EQUIPMENT

Sharp knife
Cutting board
Vegetable peeler
Measuring cup and spoons
Large skillet
Wooden spoon
Fork

*These creamy Swedish potatoes
are cooked on the stove.*

DIRECTIONS   *6 servings*

1. Have an adult help you peel the onion and chop it into small pieces. Set the onion aside.

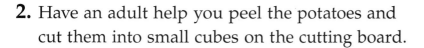
Step 1

2. Have an adult help you peel the potatoes and cut them into small cubes on the cutting board.

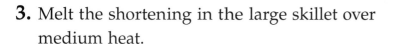
Step 2

3. Melt the shortening in the large skillet over medium heat.

4. Add the potatoes and onion. Cook them over medium heat for 10 minutes. Sprinkle them with salt and pepper and stir a few times.

5. Stir while you add the cream a little at a time. When the liquid bubbles, turn down the heat and *simmer*, or let it bubble gently, for 10 minutes.

6. Test the potatoes with a fork to see if they are cooked. If the fork goes into the potatoes easily, they are done. 💙

CABBAGE AND APPLE SALAD

This crunchy salad tastes good with ham and potatoes.

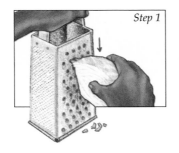

Step 1

HONEY FROM BEES

Pioneers sometimes kept bees in straw **skeps** *like this one near their homes. They used the honey to sweeten foods or to soothe sore throats, and they melted down the waxy honeycombs to make beeswax candles.*

INGREDIENTS

1/2 head cabbage, medium size
2 apples
1/2 cup raisins
1/2 cup heavy cream
1/3 cup honey

EQUIPMENT

Sharp knife
Cutting board
Grater
Large bowl
Measuring cups
Large spoon and fork
Small bowl
Plate

DIRECTIONS   *6 servings*

1. Have an adult help you cut and coarsely shred the cabbage. Then put the cabbage into the large bowl.

2. Have an adult help you cut each apple into 4 pieces and remove the apple cores. Use the grater to coarsely shred the apples into the large bowl.

3. Add the raisins to the bowl.

4. Use the large spoon and fork to toss the cabbage, apples, and raisins. Lift up some salad and let it drop. Continue doing this until the ingredients are mixed together.

5. Combine the cream and honey in the small bowl. Pour the mixture over the salad and toss it lightly.

6. Cover the bowl with the plate and put it in the refrigerator to chill before serving.

FRUIT SOUP

INGREDIENTS

8 ounces mixed dried fruit
4 cups cold water
1/2 cup raisins
1 cinnamon stick
1 tablespoon cornstarch
1/4 cup cold water

EQUIPMENT

Knife and cutting board
3-quart saucepan
Measuring cups and spoon
Wooden spoon
Ladle
Serving bowl
Small bowl

Thick fruit soup is a naturally sweet dessert that can be eaten warm or cold.

DIRECTIONS **6 servings**

1. Cut the fruit into small pieces and place them into the saucepan. Add the cold water and soak for 1 to 2 hours.

Step 1

2. Add the raisins and cinnamon stick to the fruit. Cook the mixture over medium heat until it *boils*, or bubbles quickly.

3. Lower the heat and *simmer,* or let the mixture bubble gently, for 30 minutes. Stir often so the fruit doesn't stick to the pan.

4. Have an adult ladle the hot fruit into the serving bowl. Leave the juice in the pan.

5. In the small bowl, mix the cornstarch with 1/4 cup cold water. Stir this mixture into the juice in the saucepan.

6. Heat up the juice until it boils, stirring constantly. When the juice is as thick as honey, pour it over the fruit and stir. ♥

DRYING FOODS

Pioneer families like Kirsten's preserved some foods by drying them. Berries and wild fruits were laid out on flat stones or hung from cabin rafters to dry. Then they were packed in bags or crocks until they were needed for cooking.

SWEDISH ALMOND RUSKS

Crunchy rusks, flavored with cardamom and almonds, are perfect for dipping into hot milk or coffee.

INGREDIENTS

1 cup shortening
1½ cups sugar
2 eggs
1 cup buttermilk
4 cups flour
1 teaspoon baking soda
1 teaspoon salt
1½ teaspoons ground
   cardamom
1 cup chopped almonds
Cooking oil

EQUIPMENT

Measuring cups
   and spoons
Wooden spoon
2 large mixing bowls
Small bowl
Fork
Sifter
3 small loaf pans
Toothpick
Potholders
Serrated knife
Cutting board
Spatula
3 cookie sheets

DIRECTIONS   *36 rusks*

1. Beat the shortening and sugar together in a large mixing bowl until they are creamy.

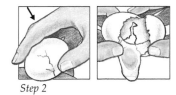

Step 2

2. Crack the eggs into the small bowl and beat them with the fork.

3. Add the beaten eggs and the buttermilk to the shortening and sugar mixture. Stir well.

Step 4

4. Put the sifter into the other large mixing bowl. Measure the flour, baking soda, salt, and cardamom into the sifter. Then sift them into the bowl. Mix in the chopped almonds.

5. Add the flour mixture 1 cup at a time to the liquid ingredients. Mix well after each addition.

6. Preheat the oven to 350°. Use cooking oil to grease the loaf pans. Spoon the batter into the loaf pans until they are about half full.

7. Bake the bread on the middle oven rack for 30 to 40 minutes. The bread is done if a toothpick inserted into the middle comes out clean. If the toothpick comes out with dough on it, bake the bread a little longer. Check it every 5 minutes.

8. Have an adult take the bread out of the oven when it is done. Turn the oven down to 200°.

9. Use a knife to loosen each loaf from the sides of the pan. Then use potholders to turn the pan upside down. Gently shake it over the cutting board until the bread falls out.

10. Let the loaves cool for 10 minutes. Cut each loaf into 12 slices slowly so it doesn't crumble. Use the spatula to move each slice to a cookie sheet after you slice it.

11. Have an adult help you put the cookie sheets into the oven. Let the slices bake for 1 to 3 minutes, checking each minute until they are dry and toasty brown.

12. Have an adult take the cookie sheets out of the oven and turn over each slice. Continue baking until the second side is toasty brown. When the rusks are done, let them cool on the cookie sheets before serving them. 💜

MORTAR AND PESTLE

*Pioneers ground spices like cardamom seeds with a mortar and pestle. A **mortar** is a sturdy bowl made of wood or stone. Pioneers used the **pestle**, a small club, to grind and mash spices and herbs in the mortar.*

Step 9

Step 10

FAVORITE FOODS

Kirsten's favorite foods were a mix of the old and the new—foods that she had enjoyed in Sweden and new foods that she and Mama learned to make in America.

At the end of a long day of work, thick potato soup with bread and cheese was a favorite supper meal for Kirsten and her family. Hearty Swedish meatballs were fun to shape into balls to cook. They were filling, too!

Sometimes Mama made thin Swedish pancakes as a supper dessert. In Sweden, a supper of pea soup and Swedish pancakes was a *custom*, or tradition. The Larsons carried on their Swedish traditions even after they had settled in America.

Mama fried the Swedish pancakes on the stove, and Kirsten served them to Papa and Lars first. Then Peter and Britta would eat. Finally, after everyone else had their fill, Kirsten and Mama sat down and enjoyed their Swedish pancakes together. Papa entertained the family with stories while Kirsten and Mama finished eating and cleaned up one more time before bed.

From Indian neighbors, early pioneers learned how to use many native American foods. For example, Indians taught pioneers to tap maple trees and boil the sap to make maple syrup.

In summer, the children picked wild berries and helped Mama make thick jams that could be preserved and eaten all year. In autumn, the family collected ripe apples. Some apples were hung in the cabin to dry. Others were cooked to make fresh applesauce.

When winter came, the Larsons looked forward to their traditional Swedish Christmas celebrations. Then Kirsten helped Mama prepare her two very favorite foods—St. Lucia buns and pepparkakor cookies!

FAVORITE FOODS

♥

Potato Soup

•

Swedish Meatballs

•

Fresh Applesauce

•

Swedish Pancakes

•

St. Lucia Buns

•

Pepparkakor Cookies

POTATO SOUP

Thick potato soup with rye bread and cheese was a hearty supper at the end of a long workday.

INGREDIENTS

3 slices of bacon
1 small onion
6 medium potatoes
1 teaspoon salt
Cold water
2 cups milk
2 tablespoons butter
$\frac{1}{8}$ teaspoon pepper

EQUIPMENT

Paper towels
Skillet
Fork
Knife
Cutting board
Vegetable peeler
Measuring cups
   and spoons
3-quart saucepan with lid
Potato masher
Wooden spoon

POTATOES

In many Swedish homes, potatoes were eaten at every meal. One book on potato cookery, published in Sweden in the 1840s, was called **The Potato Friend, an Indispensable Book for Rich and Poor, in Town as Well as in the Country.**

DIRECTIONS   *12 servings*

1. Put 2 layers of paper towels onto the counter next to the stove.

2. Separate the bacon strips and place them side by side in the skillet.

3. Turn on the heat to medium high. Have an adult help you cook the bacon slices until the edges start to curl.

4. Use the fork to turn each slice to the other side. Continue cooking, turning the slices frequently.

5. When the bacon is golden brown and crisp, lift it out of the skillet and put it onto the paper towels to cool.

6. Have an adult help you peel the onion and chop it into small pieces.

Step 6

7. Have an adult help you peel the potatoes. Cut each potato into 4 pieces.

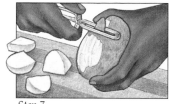
Step 7

8. Put the potatoes, onion pieces, and salt into the saucepan. Put in just enough cold water to cover them.

9. Turn the heat to medium high until the water begins to *boil,* or bubble quickly.

10. Turn down the heat. Cover the pan and let the onions and potatoes *simmer,* or bubble slowly, for about 20 minutes, or until the fork can pierce the potatoes easily.

11. Turn off the burner. Leave the cooking water in the pan. Use the potato masher to mash the potatoes and onions.

Step 11

12. Turn the burner back on medium-high heat. Add the milk slowly while you stir.

13. When the soup begins to simmer, add the butter and pepper. Crumble the bacon into the soup.

14. Keep stirring the soup while it simmers until it is smooth and hot. 💜

POTATOES FOR SURVIVAL

Sometimes new immigrants survived their first winter in America on little more than a few bushels of potatoes.

SWEDISH MEATBALLS

*Swedish pioneers often made their meatballs with ground **venison**, or deer meat, instead of ground beef.*

INGREDIENTS

2 slices of bread
1/2 cup heavy cream
1/2 cup milk
Small onion
1 tablespoon butter
1 pound lean ground beef
1/2 pound lean ground pork
1 egg
1 teaspoon salt
Dash of ground ginger, nutmeg, and pepper
2 tablespoons oil
1 tablespoon flour
1 cup cold water

EQUIPMENT

Knife
Cutting board
Small mixing bowl
Measuring cups and spoons
Skillet with lid
Large mixing bowl
Wooden spoon
Slotted spoon
Plate
Paper towels

DIRECTIONS   *6 servings*

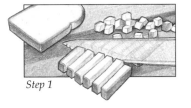

Step 1

1. Cut the bread into small cubes.

2. Combine the cream and milk in the small mixing bowl. Measure 1 1/2 cups of bread cubes into the liquid and let them soak for 5 minutes.

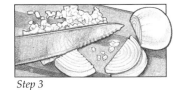

Step 3

3. Have an adult help you peel the onion and chop it into small pieces.

4. Melt 1 tablespoon of butter in the skillet over medium heat. Add the onion pieces and cook them until they are clear and tender.

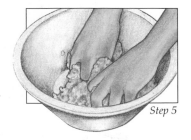

Step 5

5. Mix the ground beef and pork together in the large mixing bowl. Use a wooden spoon or use your hands—but wash your hands first!

DRYING APPLES

Pioneers often cut apples into rings and then strung them like beads to dry. Some pioneer families nailed strings of apple rings onto the sides of their houses to dry in the sun, as this picture shows. Drying the apples helped to preserve them through the winter.

8. Use the wooden spoon to stir the apples every so often to keep them from sticking to the bottom of the pan.

9. Simmer the apples for about 40 minutes, until the apples are very tender. Then turn off the heat.

10. Use the potato masher to mash the apples into a smooth, thick sauce.

Step 10

11. Stir in the cinnamon.

12. Have an adult help you spoon the applesauce into the serving bowl. You can serve the applesauce warm, or put it in the refrigerator to chill before serving. ❤

SWEDISH PANCAKES

Thin Swedish pancakes are a tasty dessert when filled with fresh jam.

INGREDIENTS

6 tablespoons butter
3 eggs
2 cups milk
1 cup flour
1/4 teaspoon salt
1 teaspoon cinnamon
1 tablespoon oil
Jam
Powdered sugar *(optional)*

EQUIPMENT

Measuring cup and spoons
Skillet
Mixing bowl
Wire whisk
Wooden spoon
Spatula
Plates

DIRECTIONS *6 servings*

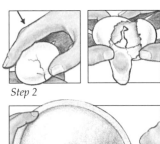

Step 2

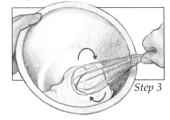

Step 3

1. Melt the butter in the skillet. Turn off the heat.

2. Crack the eggs into the mixing bowl. Use the wire whisk to beat the eggs together.

3. Add 1/2 cup of the milk to the eggs and use the wire whisk to beat the mixture for 2 minutes.

4. Add the flour to the egg mixture all at once, and use the wooden spoon to beat the mixture until it is smooth.

5. Beat in the remaining 1 1/2 cups of milk. Then add the melted butter, salt, and cinnamon.

6. Add the oil to the skillet. Ask an adult to heat up the skillet until it is very hot.

7. Drop about a tablespoon of the thin batter into the skillet for each pancake.

PIONEER COOKING UTENSILS

This man and woman are making the same kinds of cooking utensils that Kirsten and Mama used. Pioneers often carved their own spoons from wood they found near their homes. They made dippers and containers from gourds they grew themselves. And they tied willow twigs together to make whisks for beating eggs.

8. After about 1 minute, the edges of the pancakes will brown lightly. Have an adult help you turn the pancakes. Cook the other side for another minute.

9. Swedish pancakes should be eaten right away. Use the spatula to put them onto plates. Scoop a little jam onto the pancakes and roll them up. You can also sprinkle powdered sugar on top if you want. Then eat them with your fingers. Yum! 🤍

JAMS AND PRESERVES

In the 1800s, families usually made all of their own jams and preserves. Children often had the job of picking wild berries and fruits. Most children enjoyed this job because they could eat as much of the sweet wild fruit as they wanted while they filled their buckets.

ST. LUCIA BUNS

These Swedish buns are rolled and coiled into shape before baking.

ST. LUCIA DAY

Swedish immigrant families like Kirsten's celebrated holidays in their new American homes just as they had in Sweden. The traditional Swedish Yule celebration begins with St. Lucia Day on December 13 to mark the longest winter night. In the darkness before dawn, the oldest daughter goes from room to room with a tray of coffee and treats, such as St. Lucia buns.

From the book *Kirsten's Surprise*

INGREDIENTS

1/3 cup milk
1/4 cup butter
1/4 cup lukewarm water
1 package dry yeast
1/4 cup sugar
1 egg
1/2 teaspoon salt
1/4 teaspoon saffron
2 3/4 cups flour
1 tablespoon cooking oil
1 egg
1 tablespoon water
24 raisins

EQUIPMENT

Measuring cups
  and spoons
Small saucepan
Knife
Cutting board
Wooden spoon
Large mixing bowl
Clean kitchen towel
Greased cookie sheet
Fork
Small bowl
Pastry brush
Potholders
Wire cooling rack

DIRECTIONS   *6 buns*

1. Warm the milk in the small saucepan over low heat. Cut the butter into small pieces. Add the butter pieces to the warm milk and stir. Then turn off the heat.

2. Measure the lukewarm water into the large mixing bowl. Sprinkle the yeast over the water. Stir well. Set the bowl aside for 5 minutes.

3. Add the warm milk and melted butter to the yeast. Stir in the sugar, egg, salt, and saffron. Then add 1 1/2 cups flour and stir until smooth.

4. Add enough of the remaining flour so that you can shape the dough into a ball. Save some of the remaining flour for kneading the dough.

5. Put the dough on the floured cutting board. Dust your hands with flour and knead the dough *(see page 13)*. Add flour when the dough gets sticky.

6. After 5 to 10 minutes of kneading, you will have a smooth ball of dough. It should spring back when you poke it with your finger. Cover the dough with the towel and let it rest while you wash and dry the mixing bowl.

7. Spread cooking oil in the large bowl. Roll the dough in the oil until it is coated. Cover the bowl with the towel and set it in a warm place to rise. After 45 minutes, the dough should be twice as large. If not, check it again in 15 minutes.

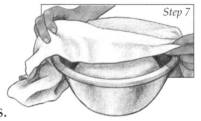
Step 7

8. Punch down the dough. Then divide it into 6 sections. Take 1 section and divide it in half. Roll each half into an 8-inch rope. Cross the 2 ropes in the middle. Then coil the ends in tight circles. Shape 5 more buns in the same way.

Step 8

9. Place the buns 2 inches apart on a greased cookie sheet. Cover with the towel. Let the buns rise for 30 to 45 minutes until they double in size. Preheat the oven to 350° while they are rising.

10. Mix the egg and water with the fork in the small bowl. Brush this mixture lightly over the top of each bun. Decorate the buns with raisins.

Step 10

11. Bake the buns for 15 to 20 minutes. When the buns are golden brown, have an adult move them to the wire rack to cool. ❤

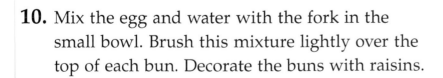

PLAN A PIONEER PARTY

MAKING WORK FUN

These people are working together to harvest crops, just as pioneers did in Kirsten's time. Pioneers worked very hard, but they tried to make their work fun by doing it with other family members or friends. Pioneers helped one another with difficult jobs like building houses and barns or plowing roads. And they also helped with tiring jobs like husking corn, cracking walnuts, and preserving food.

Pioneers worked hard to survive. They did not have time for many parties. Instead, pioneers often invited their neighbors to a work-play party, or *bee*, to work, eat, and enjoy one another's company. Here are some ideas to help you plan a pioneer bee that includes a potluck meal.

♥ WINTER BAKING BEE

The Yule season was a special time for immigrants like Kirsten and her family. They baked traditional foods to share with friends and neighbors.

Invite your guests to a baking bee. You can use the recipes for pepparkakor cookies and St. Lucia buns in this cookbook. Or you can use your own family's traditional recipes for holiday baking.

Ask each guest to bring an apron and a mixing bowl, baking utensil, or baking pan. That's what the pioneers did! Send each guest home with a small basket of baked goods that you have made together.

♥ SPRING GARDENING BEE

When spring arrived and the days grew longer, children like Kirsten and Peter often planted vegetables in the family garden.

Invite your guests to a gardening bee. If you have an outdoor garden, invite guests to help hoe and plant seeds. Or plan a gardening bee indoors using small seed pots, soil, and packets of seeds. Give each guest a plant to grow at home.

❤ SUMMER BERRY BEE

When wild berries ripened in summer, pioneer children picked as many buckets as they could. Then they helped make jams, jellies, and preserves to enjoy throughout the year.

Invite your guests to a berry bee. You can pick your own berries if you know of a berry patch or a local "pick-your-own" farm. Or you can buy berries at a fruit stand or store. To make jam from the berries, follow the directions on packages of pectin that are sold in grocery stores. Ask each guest to bring an apron, a container for picking, and a small glass jar with a lid. Send each guest home with a jar of homemade jam.

❤ FALL APPLE BEE

In the fall, pioneer farmers like the Larsons harvested crops, butchered meat, and preserved food for winter. Children like Kirsten often picked apples to make applesauce or dried apples.

Invite your guests to an apple bee. You can pick your own apples at an orchard or buy them at a fruit stand or store. Follow the directions in this cookbook to make cabbage and apple salad or applesauce. Ask each guest to bring an apron, a small container with a lid, a paring knife, and a vegetable peeler or apple corer. Each guest can take home a container of salad or applesauce.

WORKING AND PLAYING

A pioneer bee was not all work. Friends talked, sang, gossiped, and told stories as they worked. And after the work was done, everyone enjoyed a hearty meal served on tables made from wooden boards.

SHARING THE FUN

After eating, pioneers played games and held contests. Musicians played lively dance music. Everyone—young and old—joined in the fun.

POTLUCK MEAL

When pioneers finished their work bee, they usually enjoyed sharing a meal. Often each family who came to the bee brought a dish to share for a potluck meal.

Food

You can use recipes from this cookbook to prepare some traditional Swedish foods. If you plan a potluck, you can send recipes with your invitations. Or, instead of a meal, you might want to serve simple sandwiches, cheese and bread, or a dessert.

Place Settings

Most pioneers did not have enough dishes to serve a large group. Ask your guests to bring their own plates, cups, and eating utensils just as the pioneers did. It will make a colorful table!

Decorations

Pioneers often decorated with simple things found outside. Use pine boughs, pinecones, greens, grasses, and dried or fresh flowers to decorate the room or table.

Clothes

Girls can wear long skirts, aprons, or kerchiefs. Boys might wear pants with suspenders or shirts with vests. If it's warm, go barefoot. Pioneer children usually saved their shoes for cold weather!

Music

Listen to lively fiddle music while you work and eat. Your local librarian can help you find a record, tape, or CD to borrow for your pioneer bee.

AMERICAN GIRLS PASTIMES™
Activities from the Past for Girls of Today

You'll enjoy all the Pastimes books about your favorite characters in The American Girls Collection®.

Learn to cook foods that Felicity, Kirsten, Addy, Samantha, and Molly loved with the Pastimes **COOKBOOKS.** They're filled with great recipes and fun party ideas.

Make the same crafts that your favorite American Girls character made. Each of the **CRAFT BOOKS** has simple step-by-step instructions and fascinating historical facts.

Imagine that you are your favorite American Girls character as you stage a play about her. Each of the **THEATER KITS** has four Play Scripts and a Director's Guide.

Learn about fashions of the past as you cut out the ten outfits in each of the **PAPER DOLL KITS.** Each kit also contains a make-it-yourself book plus historical fun facts.

There are **CRAFT KITS** for each character with directions and supplies to make 3 crafts from the Pastimes Craft Books. Craft Kits are available only through Pleasant Company's catalogue, which you can request by filling out the postcard below.

Turn the page to learn more about the other delights in The American Girls Collection. ⟶

I'm an American girl who loves to get mail. Please send me a catalogue of The American Girls Collection®:

My name is _____

My address is _____

City _____ State _____ Zip _____

Parent's signature _____

And send a catalogue to my friend:

My friend's name is _____

Address _____

City _____ State _____ Zip _____

THE AMERICAN GIRLS COLLECTION®

The American Girls Collection tells the stories of five lively nine-year-old girls who lived long ago—Felicity, Kirsten, Addy, Samantha, and Molly. You can read about their adventures in a series of beautifully illustrated books of historical fiction. By reading these books, you'll learn what growing up was like in times past.

There is also a lovable doll for each character with beautiful clothes and lots of wonderful accessories. The dolls and their accessories make the stories of the past come alive today for American girls like you.

The American Girls Collection is for you if you love to curl up with a good book. It's for you if you like to play with dolls and act out stories. It's for you if you want something so special that you will treasure it for years to come.

To learn more about The American Girls Collection, fill out the postcard on the other side of the page and mail it to Pleasant Company, or call **1-800-845-0005.** We will send you a free catalogue about all the books, dolls, dresses, and other delights in The American Girls Collection.